A is for ant

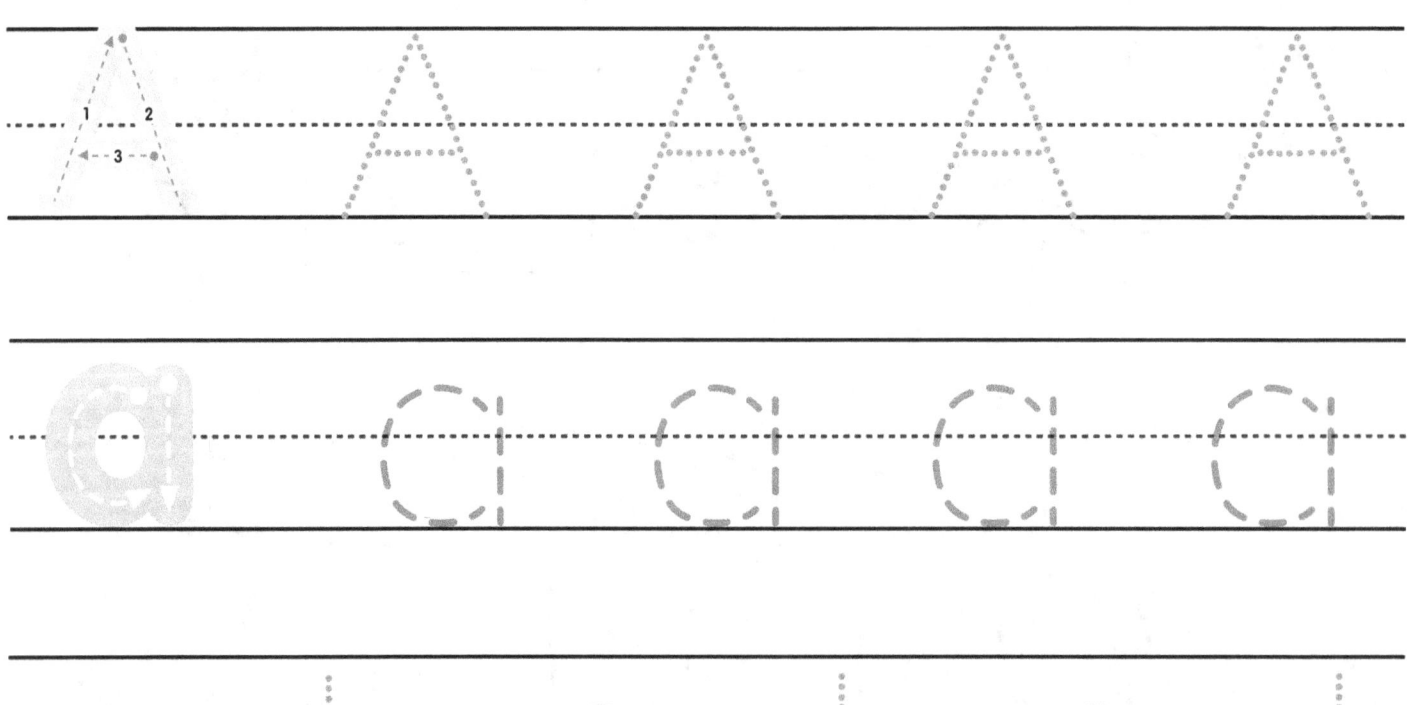

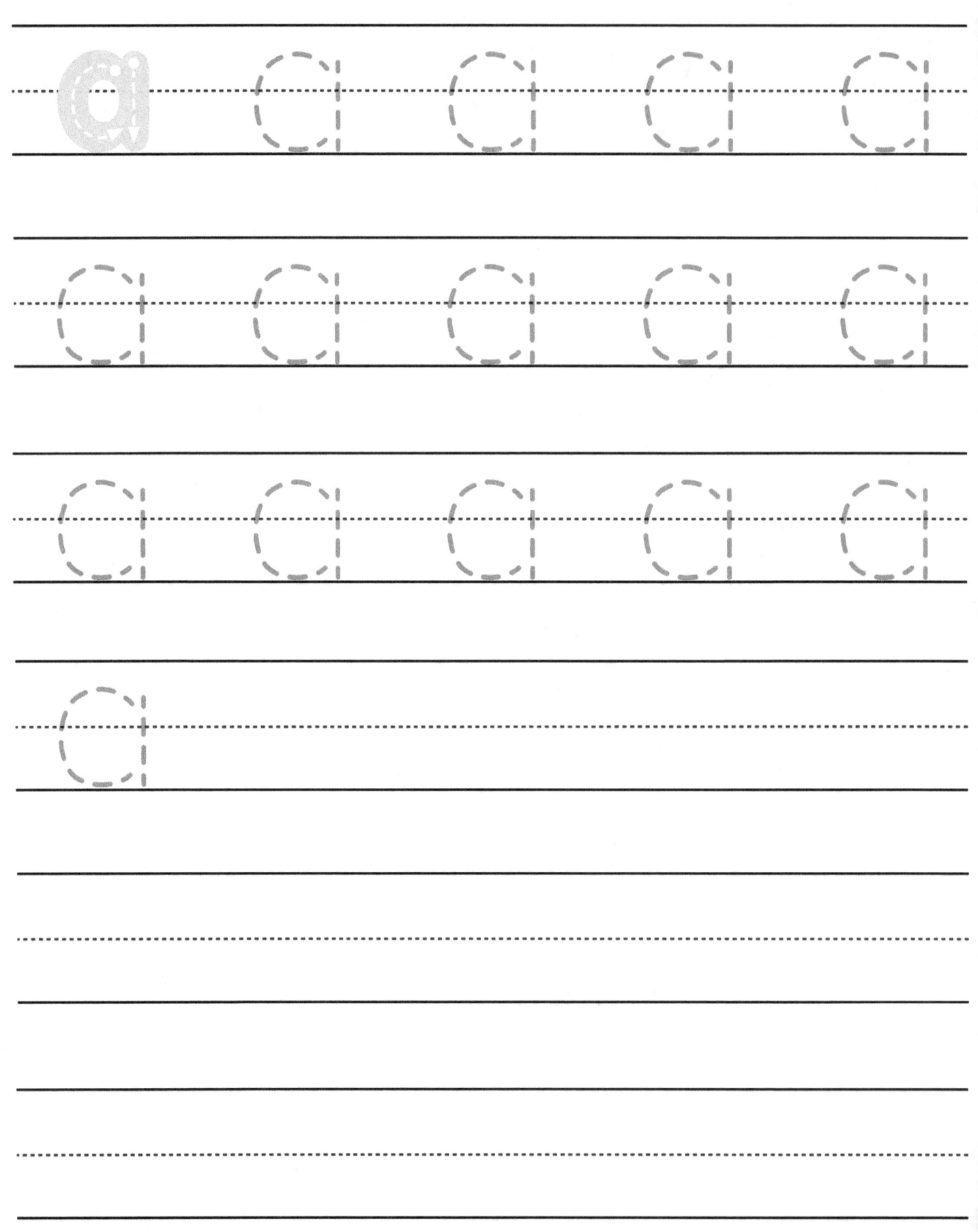

ant ant ant

ant ant ant

ant ant ant

ant

B is for bird

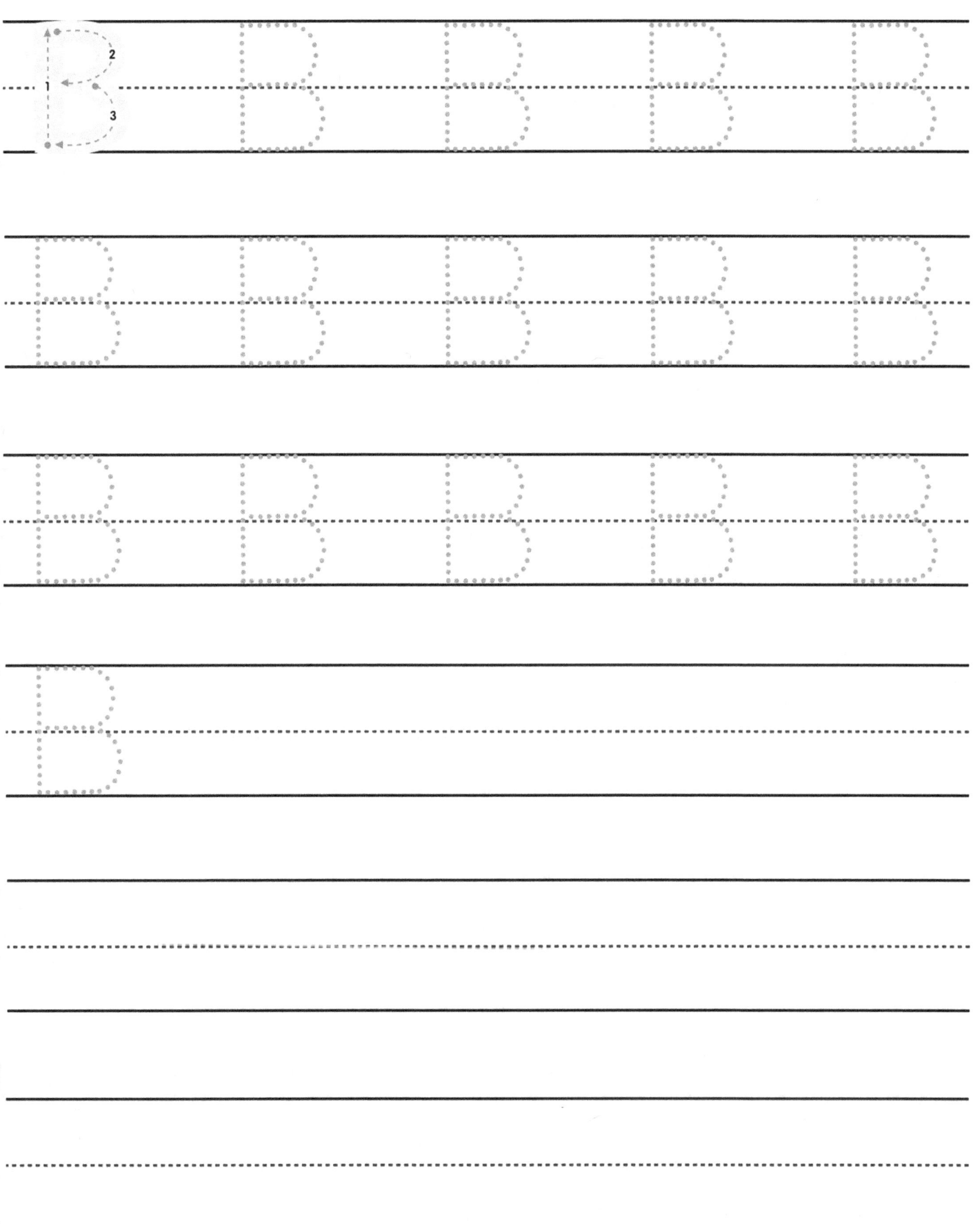

bird   bird

bird   bird

bird   bird

bird

C is for

cat

C C C C C

c c c c c c c

cat cat cat

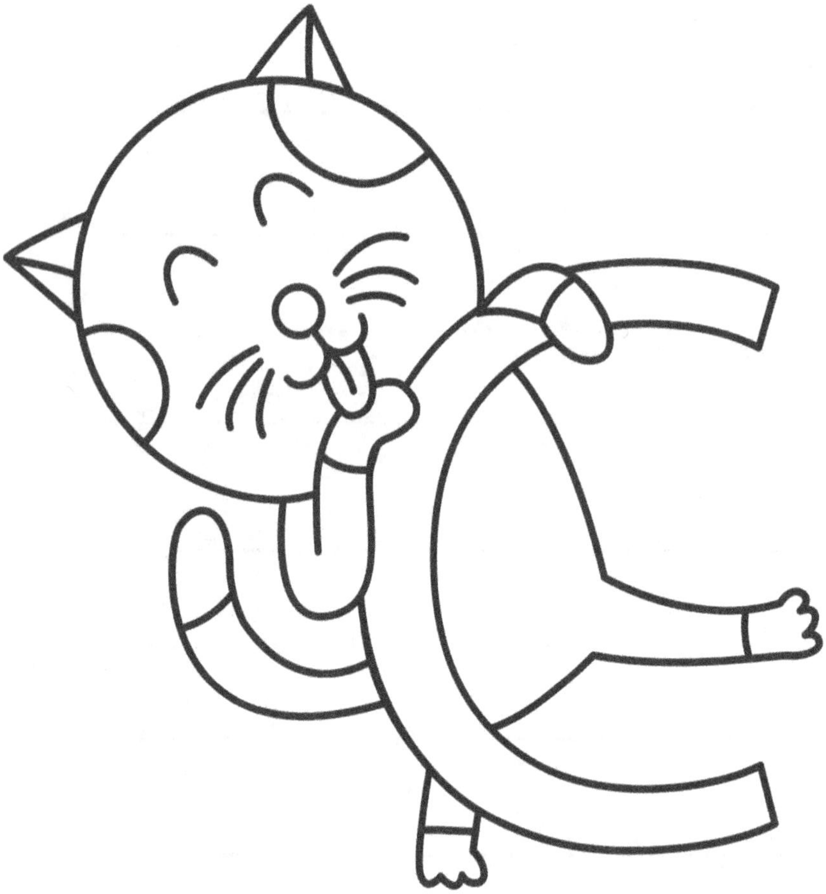

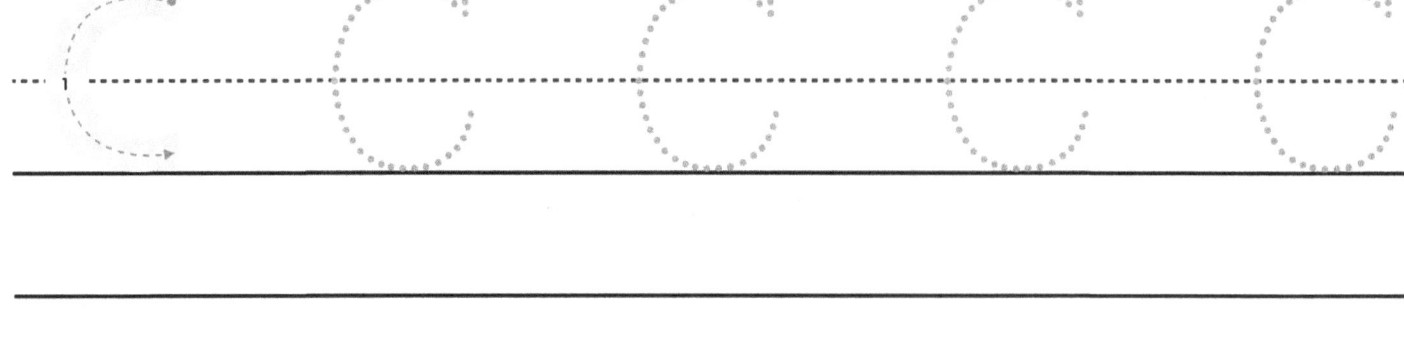

cat   cat   cat

cat   cat   cat

cat   cat   cat

cat

D is for

Dog

dog dog dog dog dog

dog dog dog dog dog

dog dog dog dog dog

dog dog

E is for

Elephant

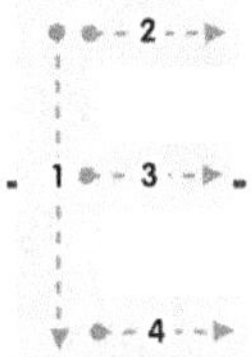

E E E E

E E E E E

E E E E E

E

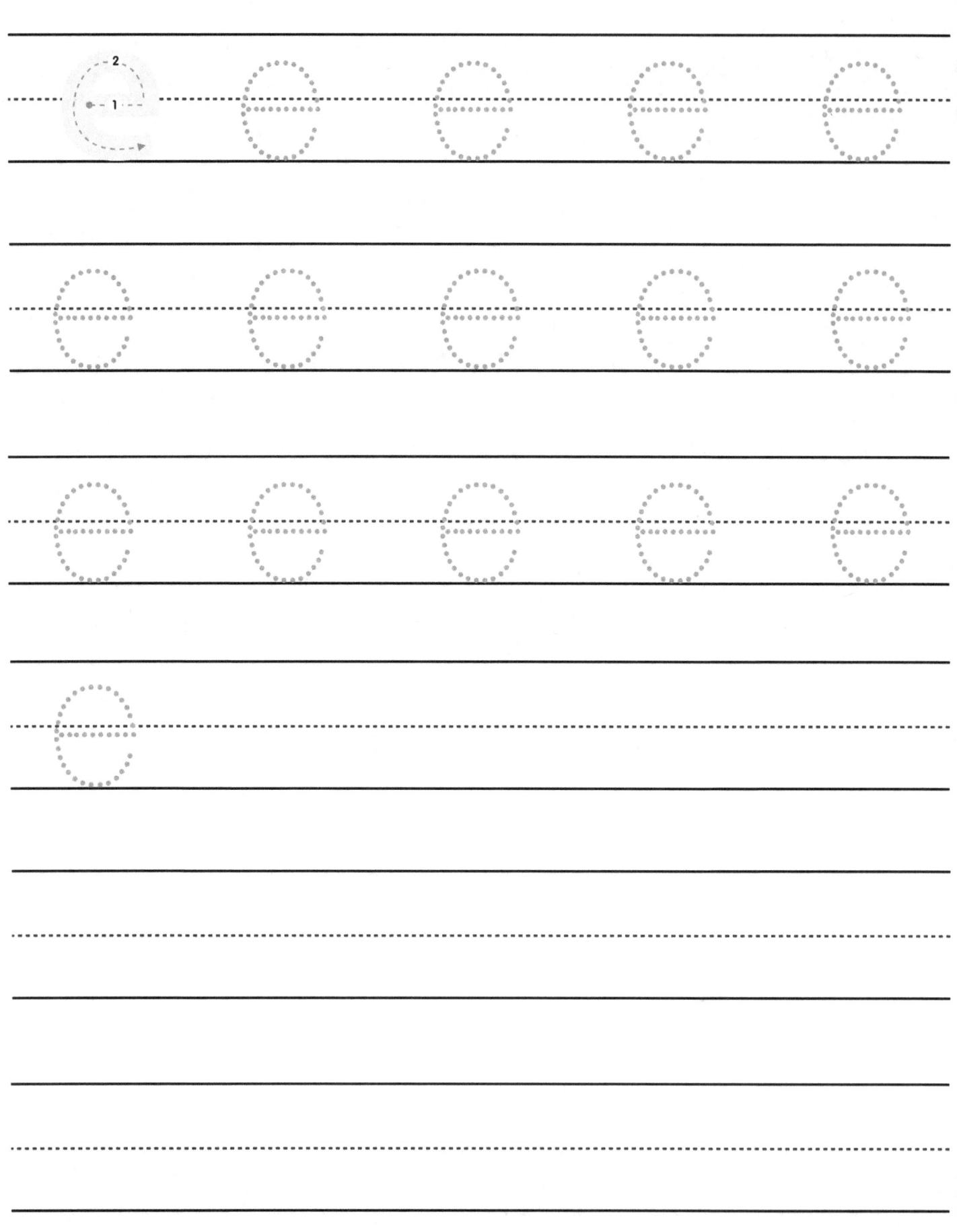

elephant

elephant

elephant

F is for Frog

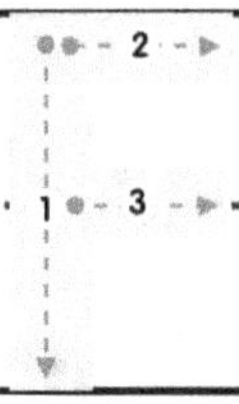

F F F F

F F F F F

F F F F F

F

frog   frog

frog   frog

frog   frog

G is for Giraffe

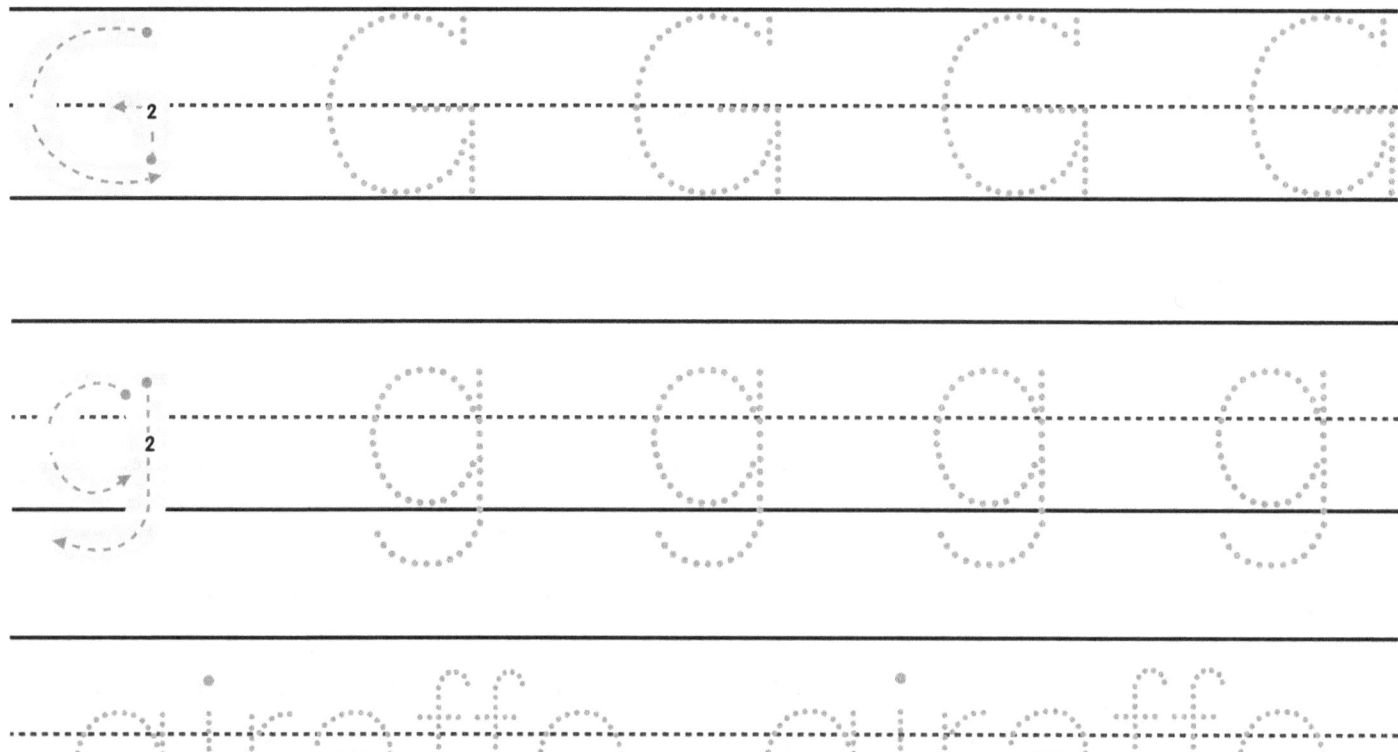

giraffe   giraffe

giraffe   giraffe

giraffe   giraffe

H is for
Hippo

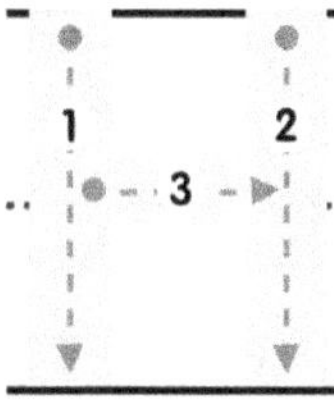
1
2
3

hippo hippo

hippo hippo

hippo hippo

I is for

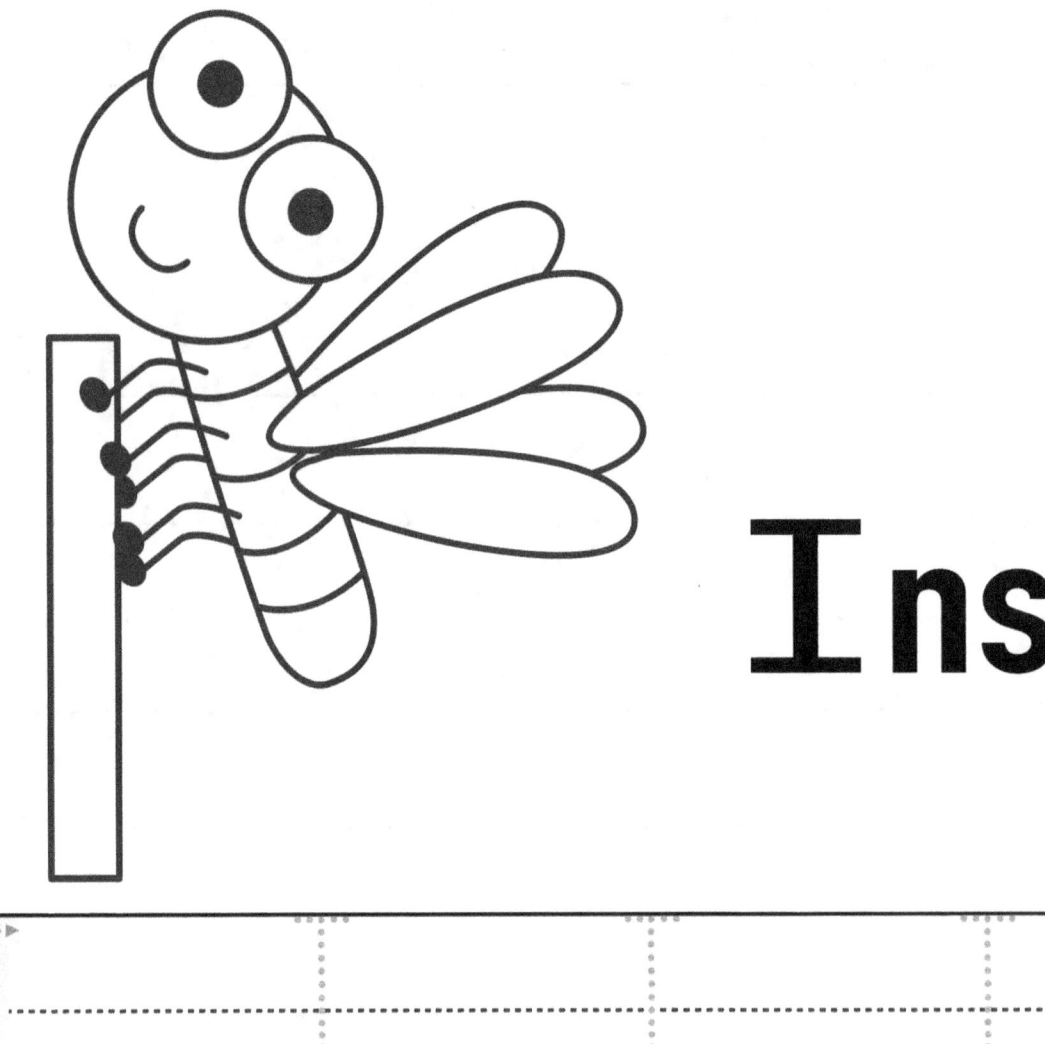

Insect

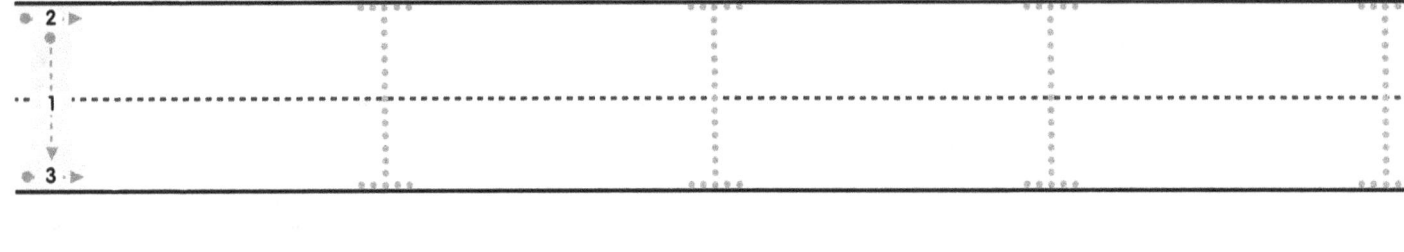

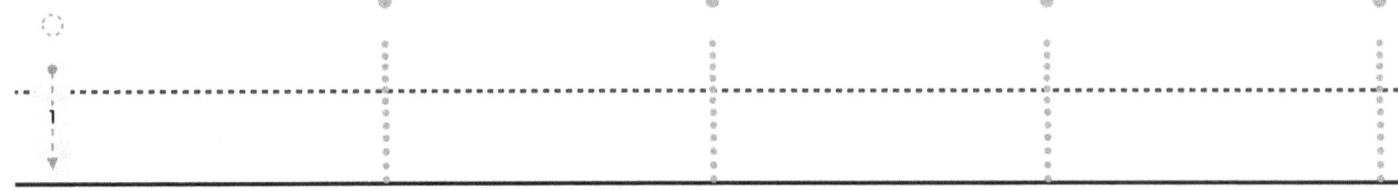

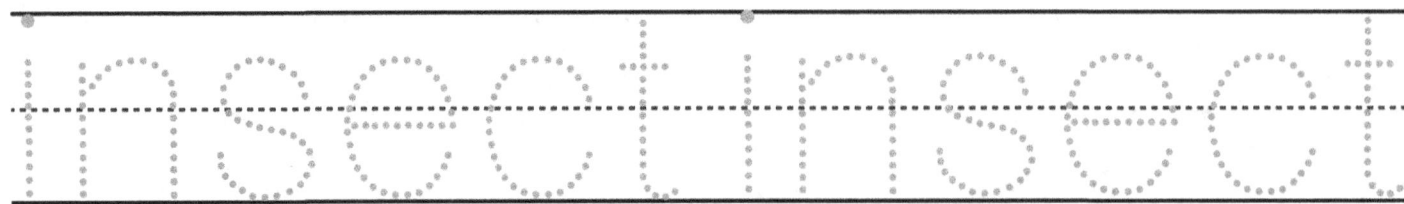

insect insect

insect insect

insect insect

J is for

J nsect

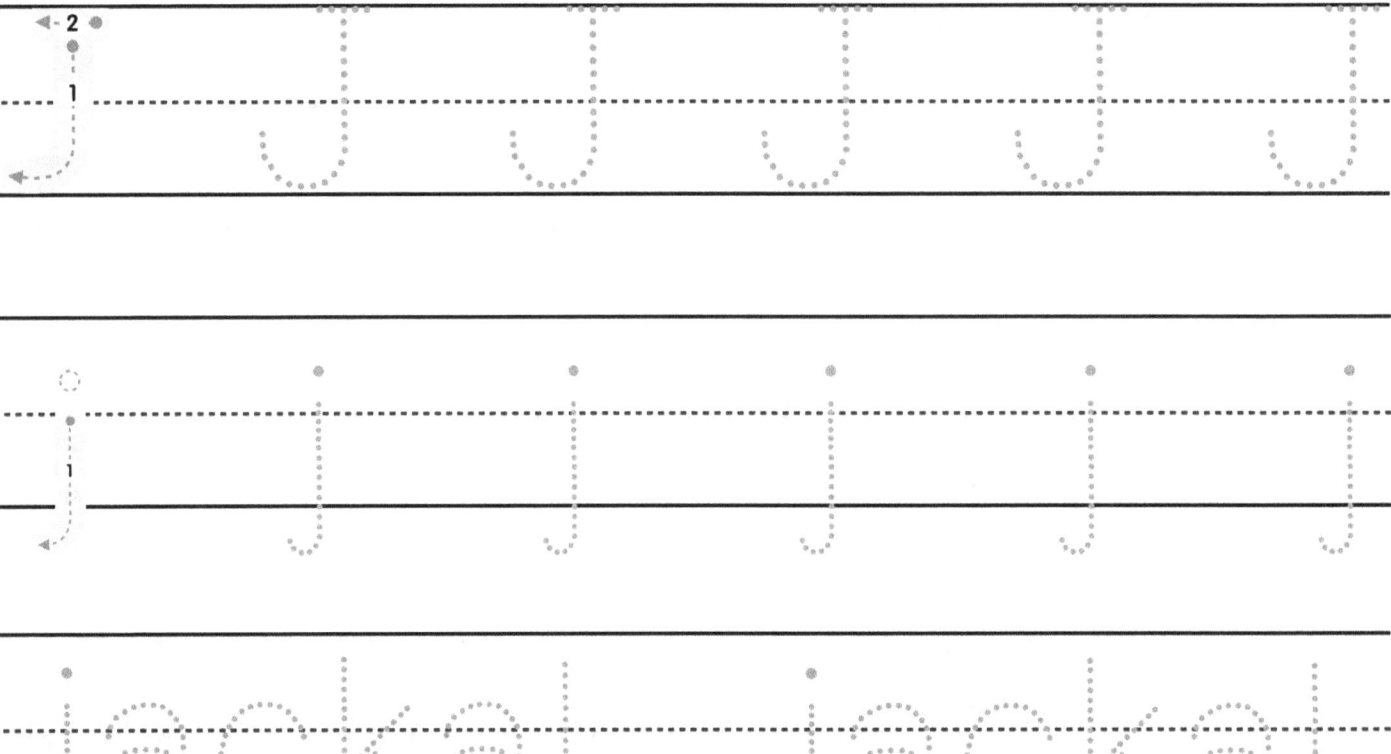

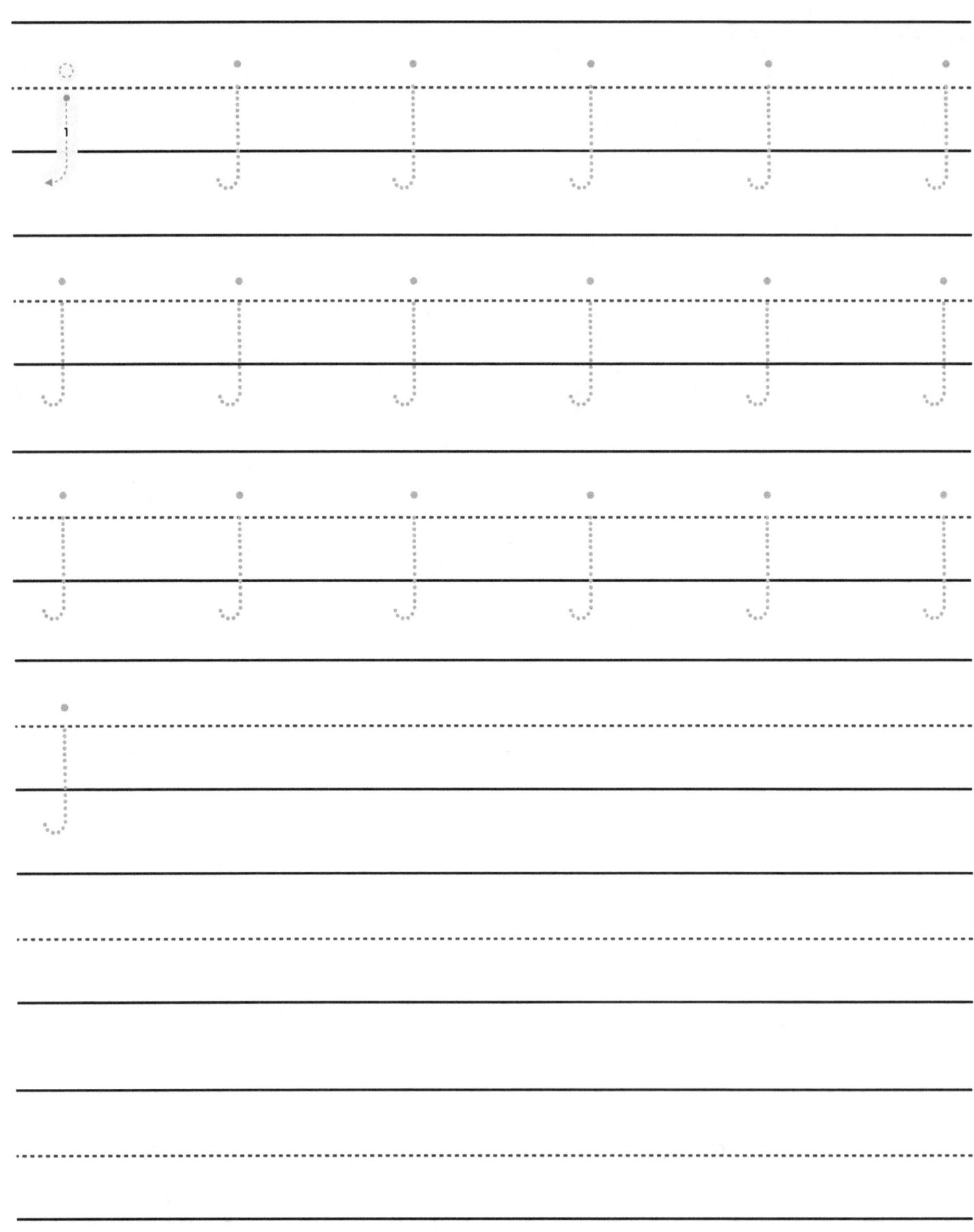

jackal jackal

jackal jackal

jackal jackal

K is for

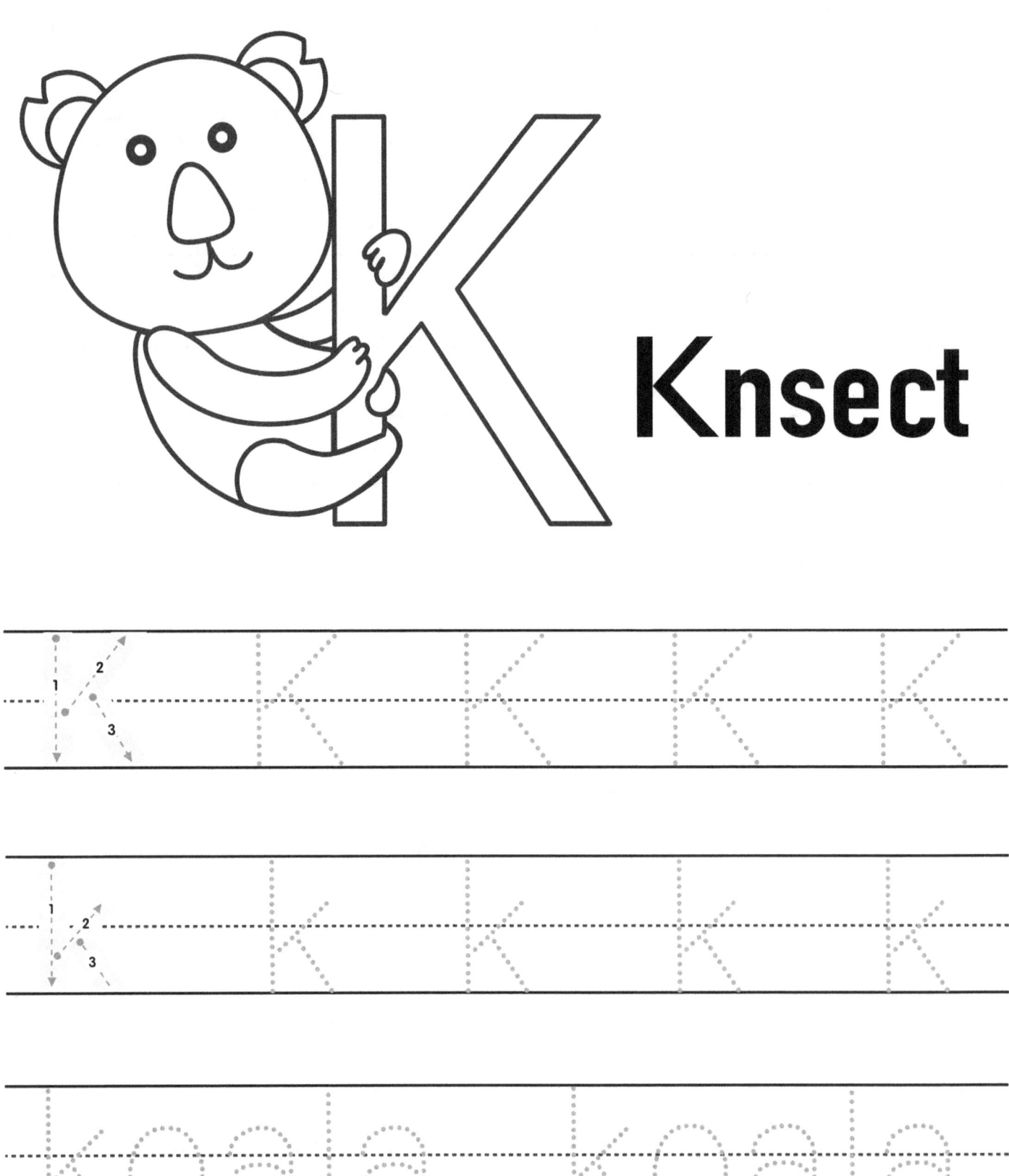

Knsect

koala koala

koala koala

koala koala

L is for
Lion

lion lion lion

lion lion lion

lion lion lion

M is for

Monkey

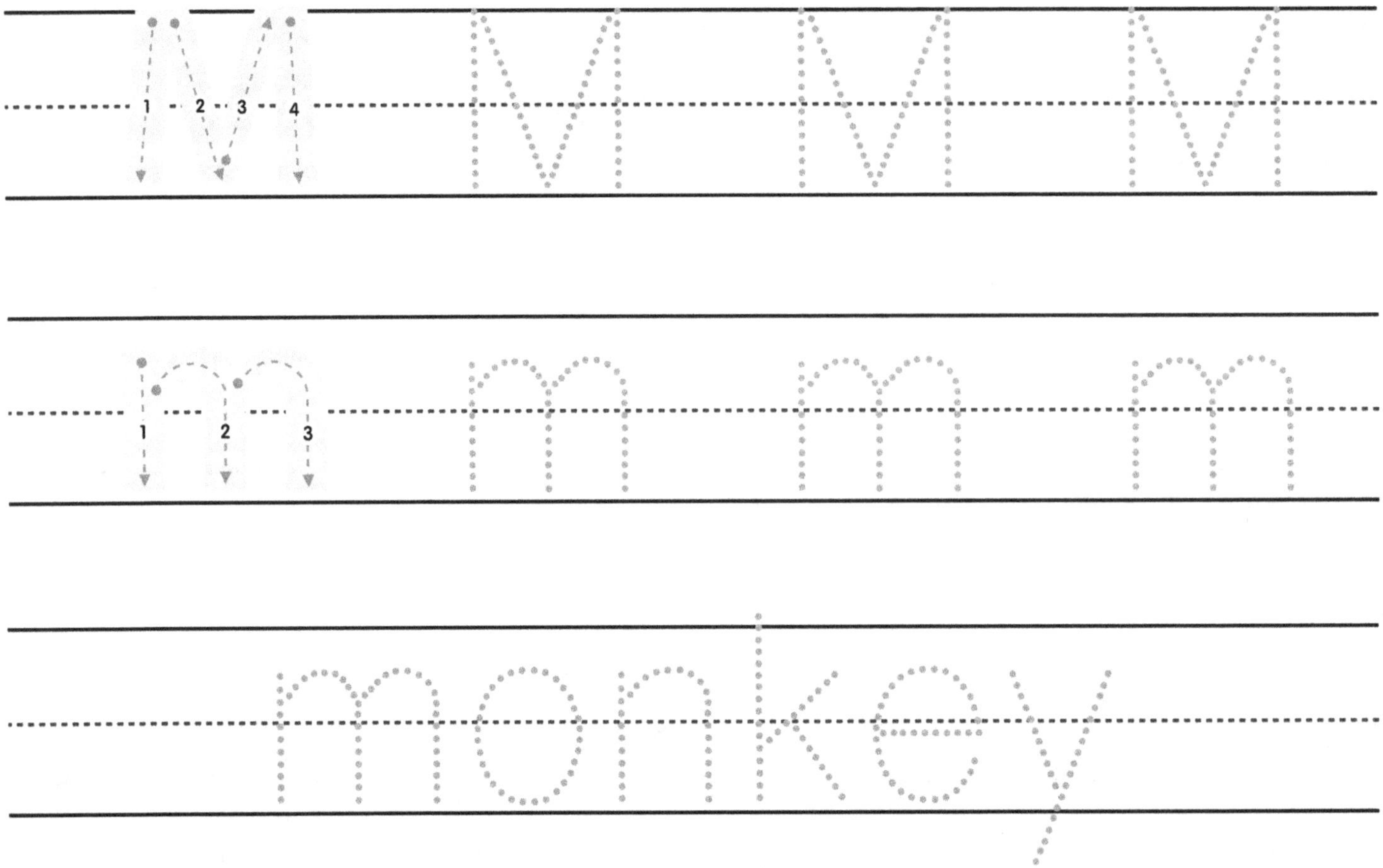

M M M M

m m m m

monkey

monkey

monkey

monkey

N is for

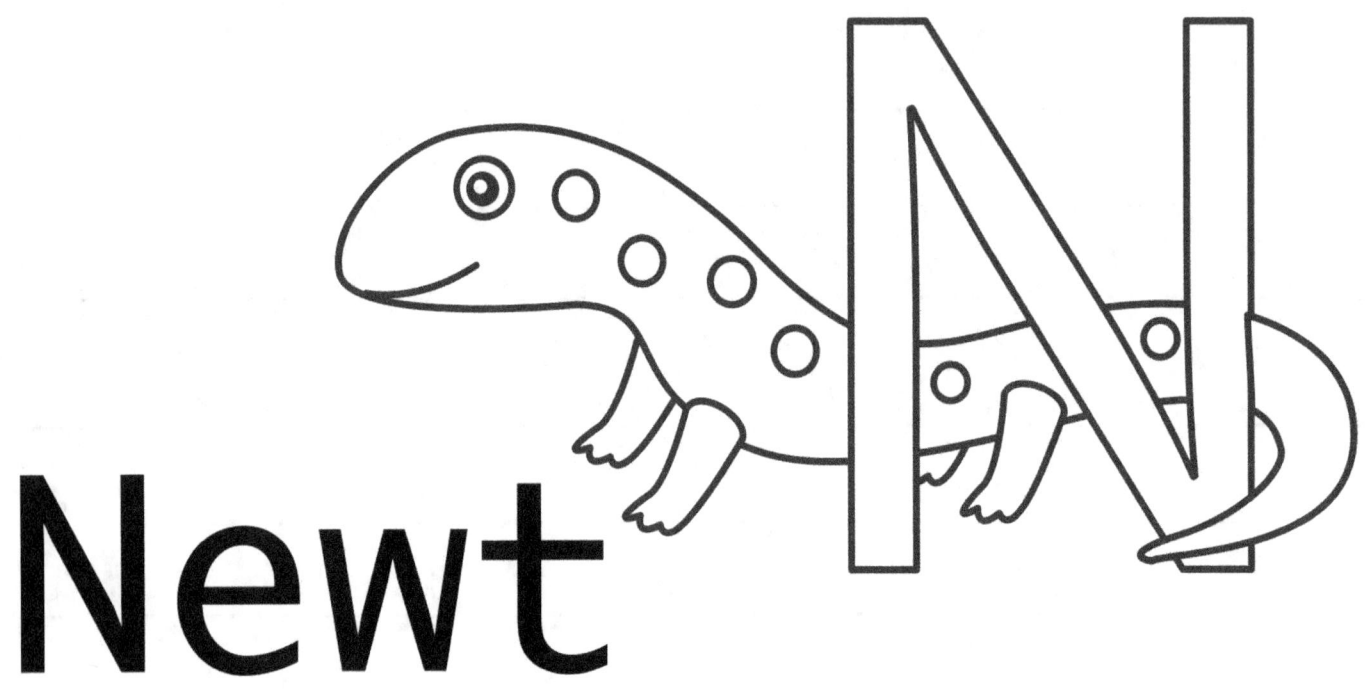

Newt

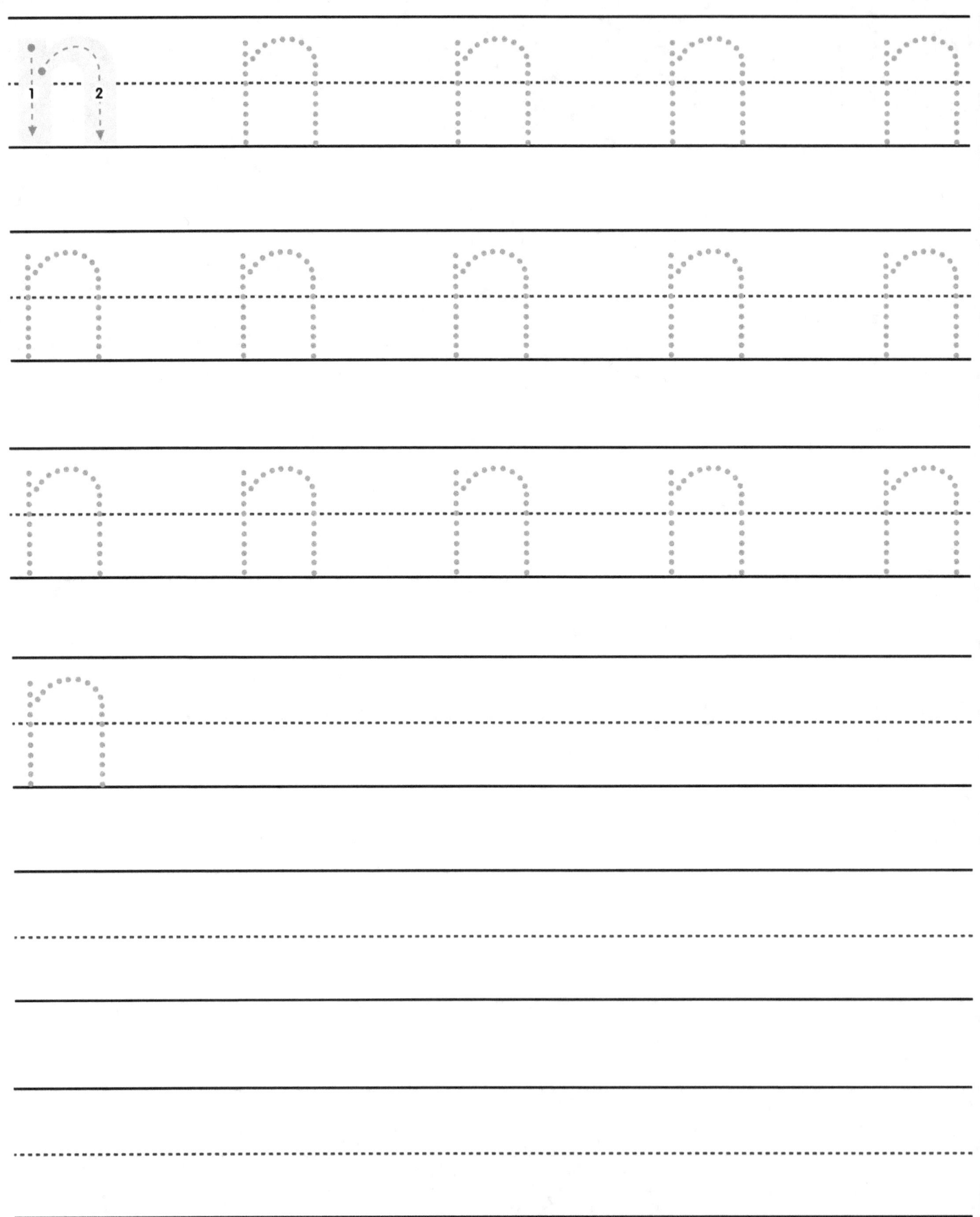

O is for

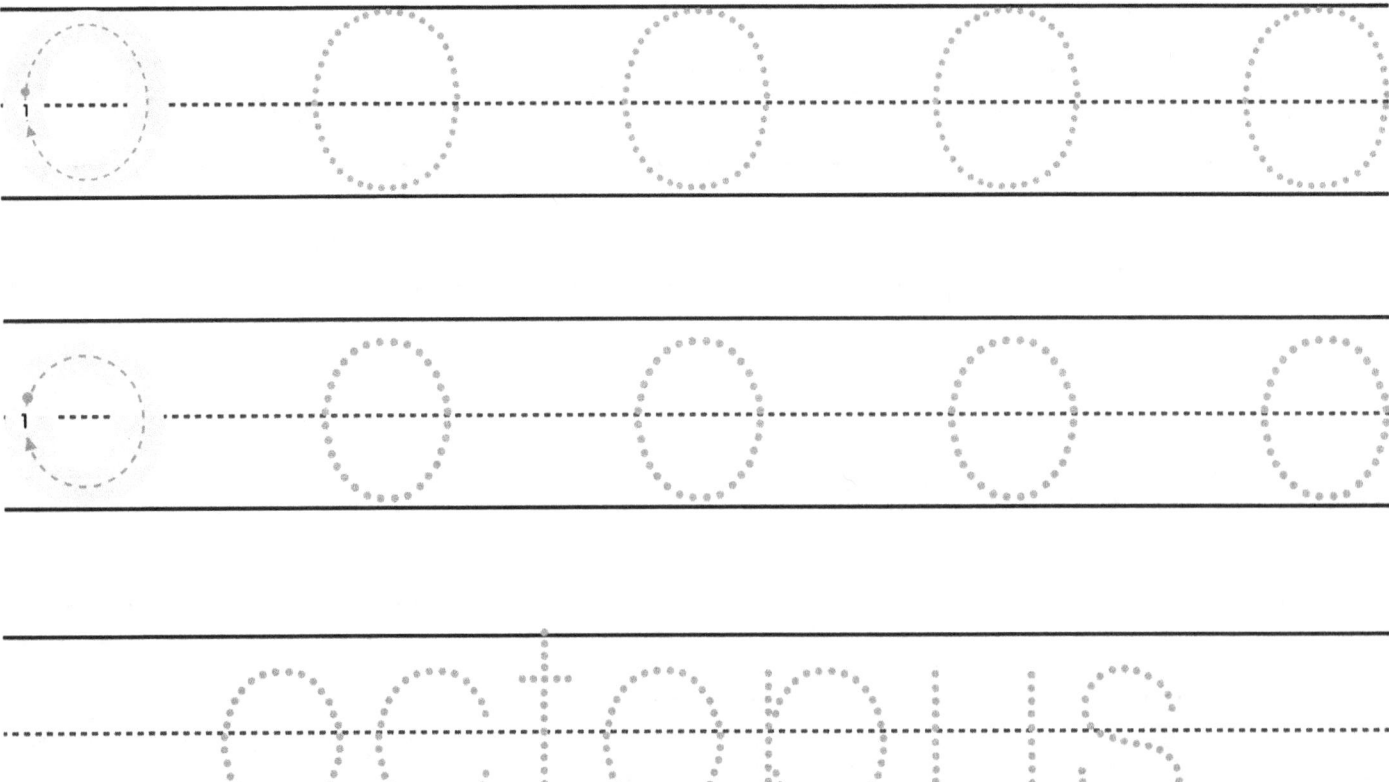

Octopus

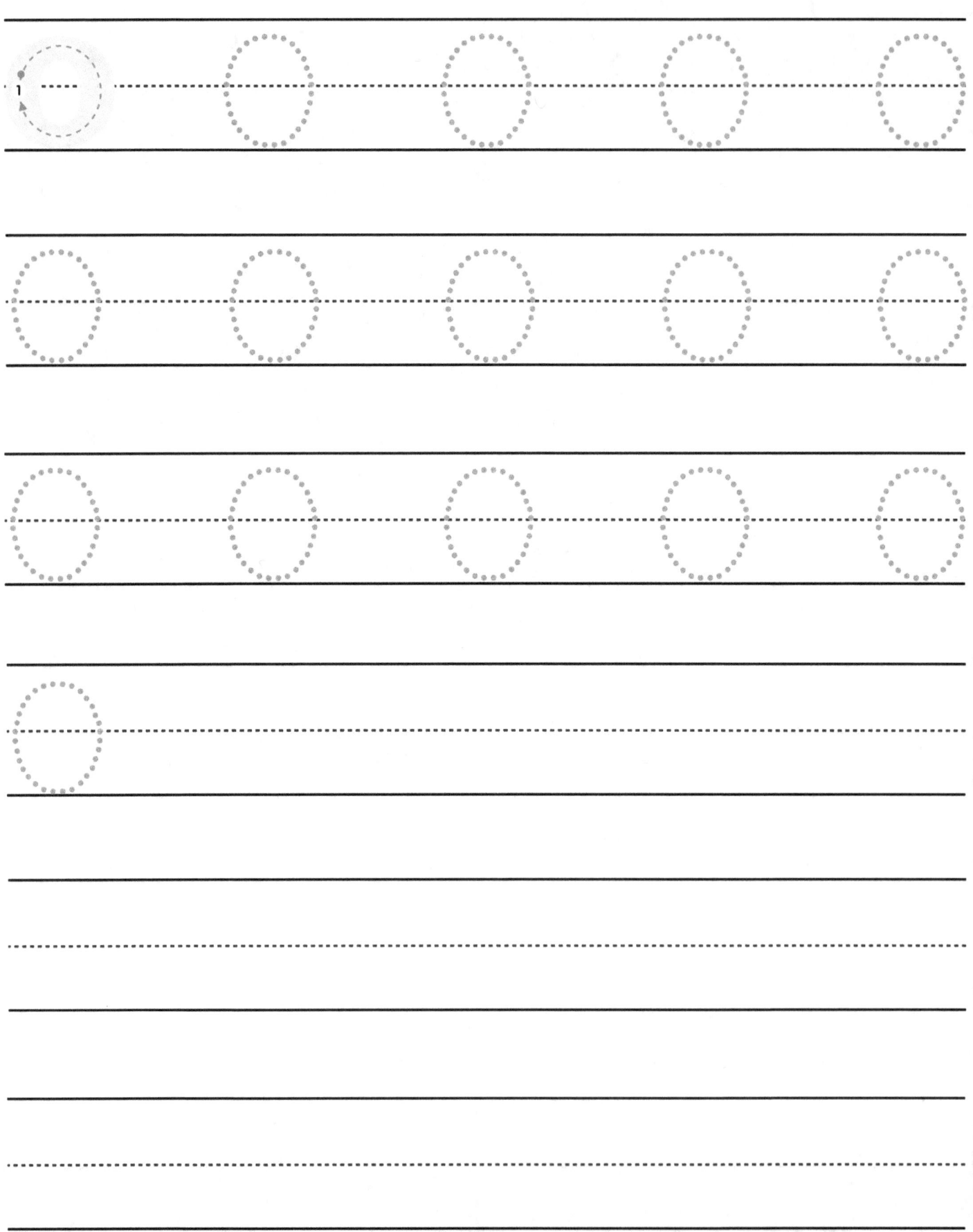

P is for
Panda

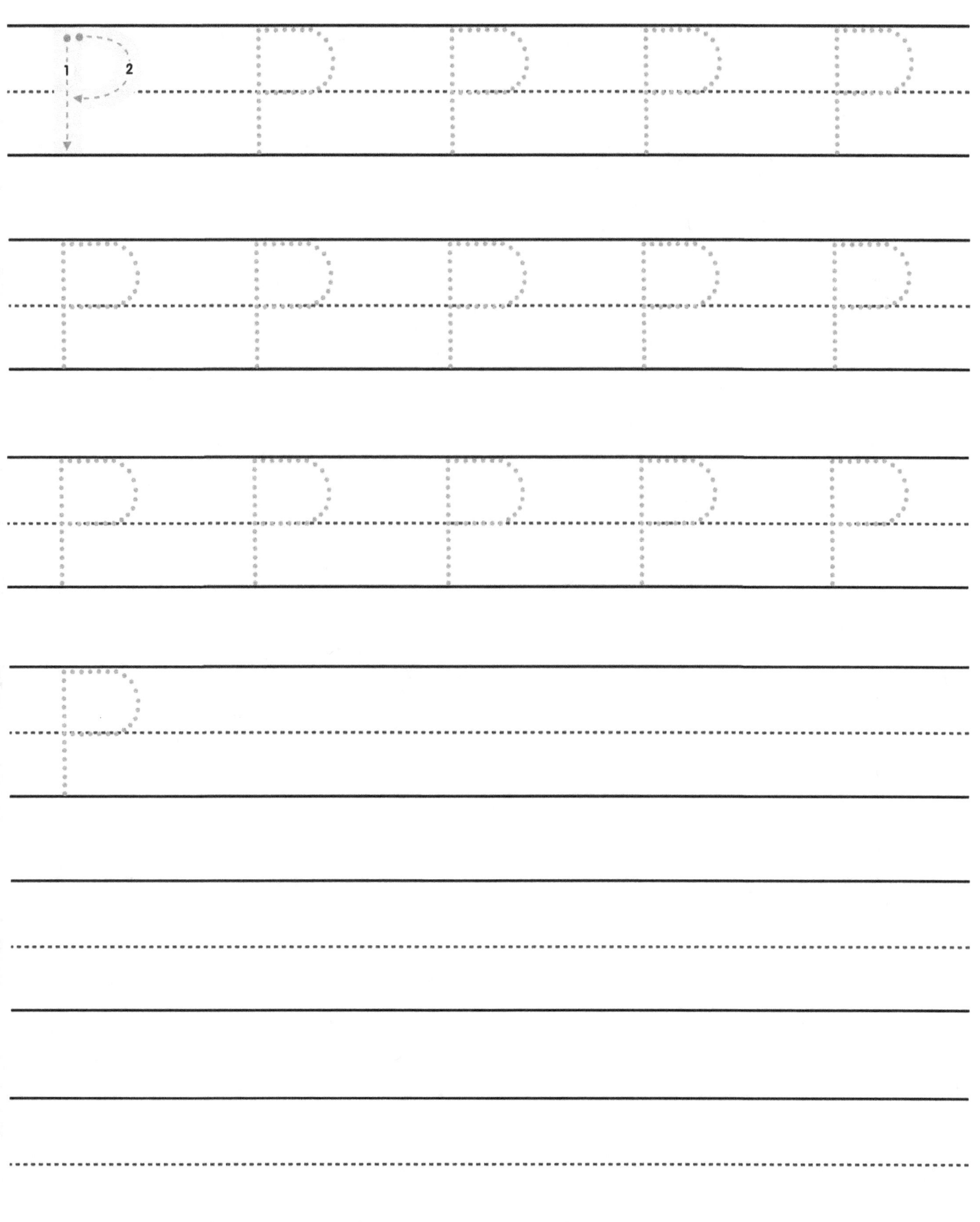

pandapanda

pandapanda

pandapanda

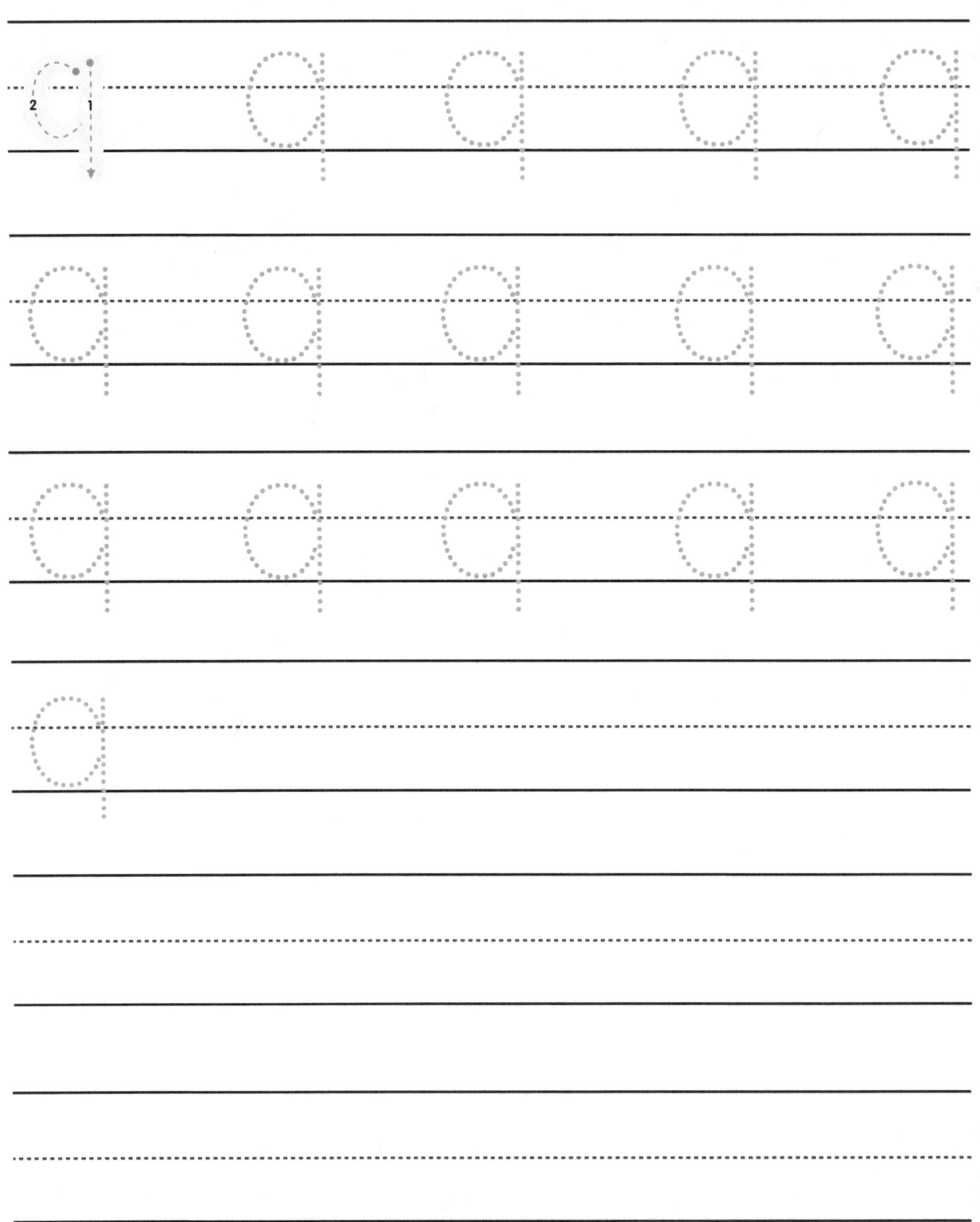

quail quail

quail quail

quail quail

R is for
Rabbit

R R R R R

r r r r

rabbit rabbit

rabbit   rabbit

rabbit   rabbit

rabbit   rabbit

S is for Sloth

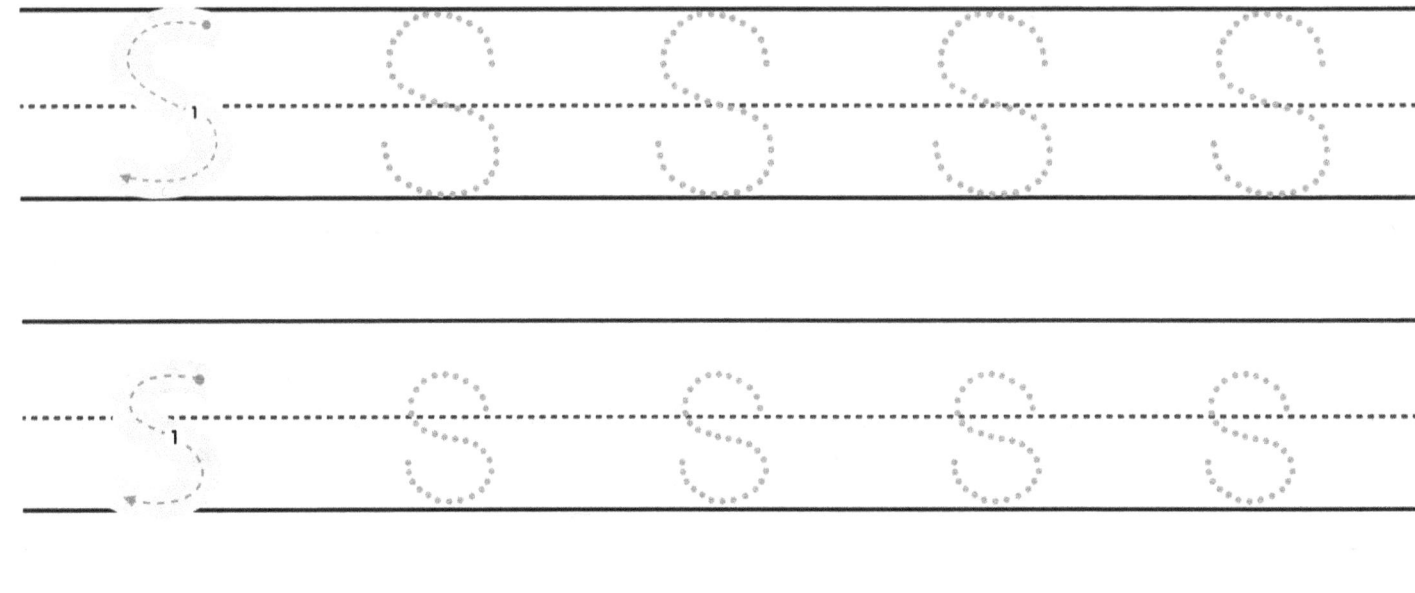

sloth   sloth

sloth   sloth

sloth   sloth

T is for
Tapir

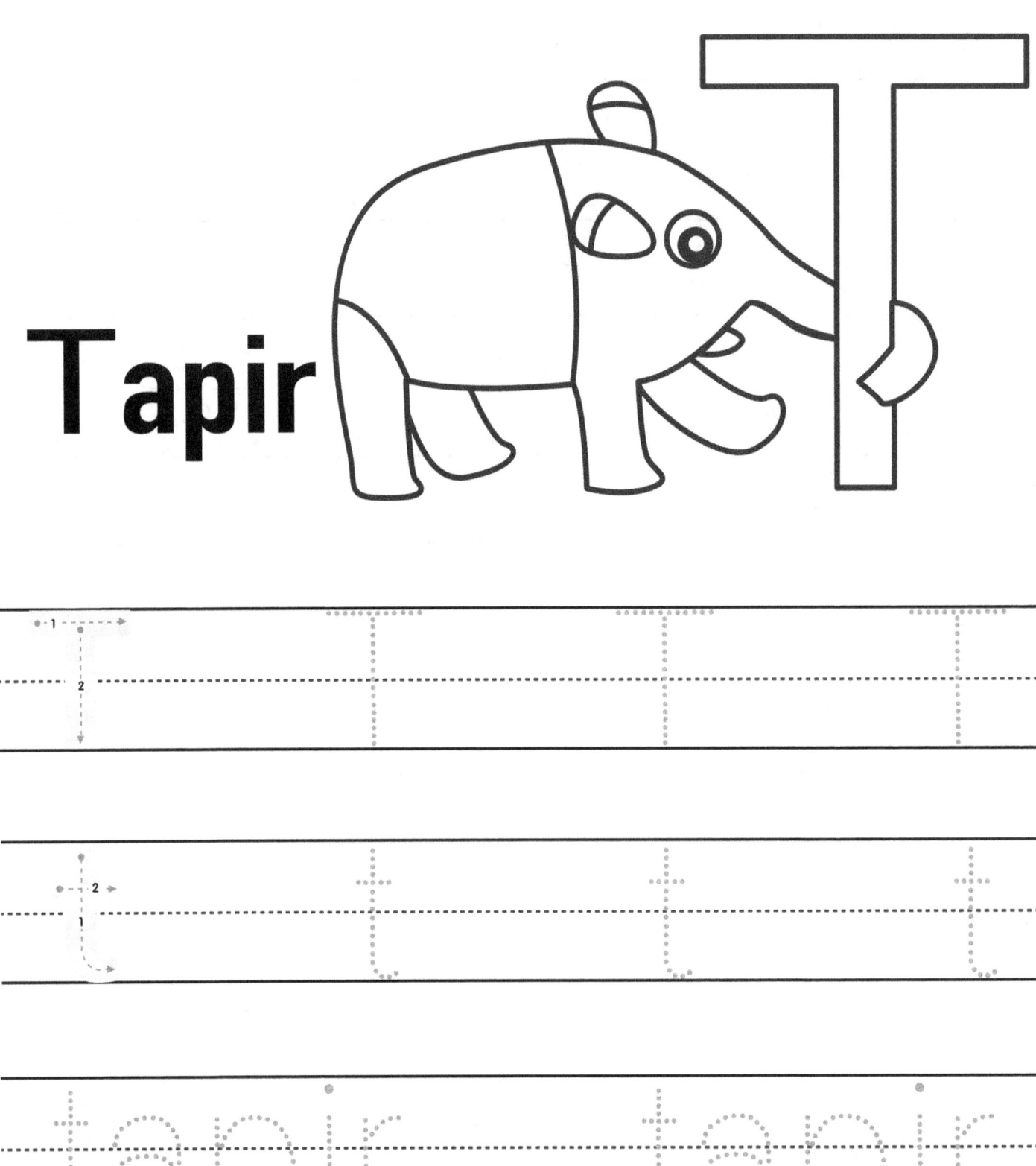

T

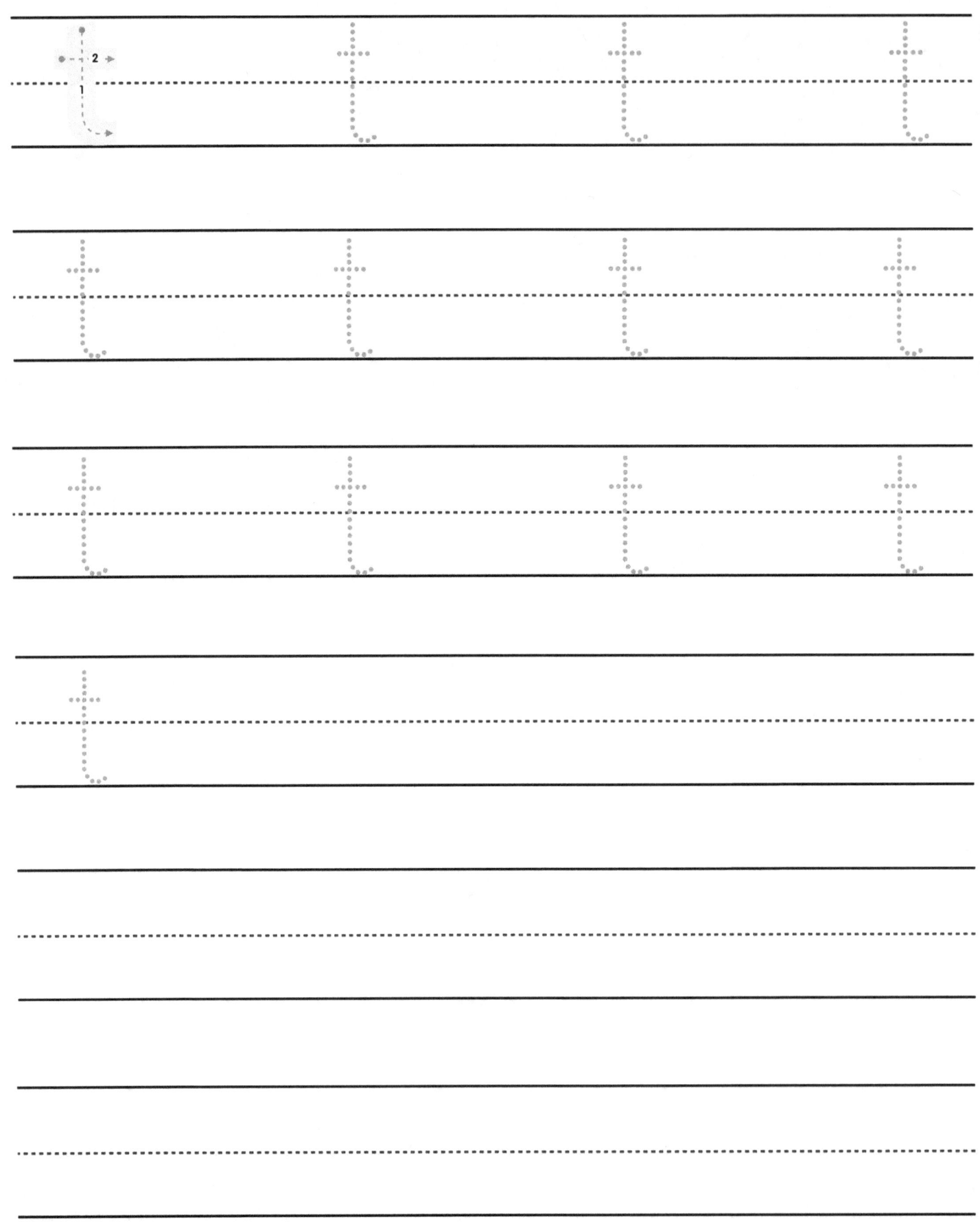

tapir   tapir

tapir   tapir

tapir   tapir

U is for

Uguisu

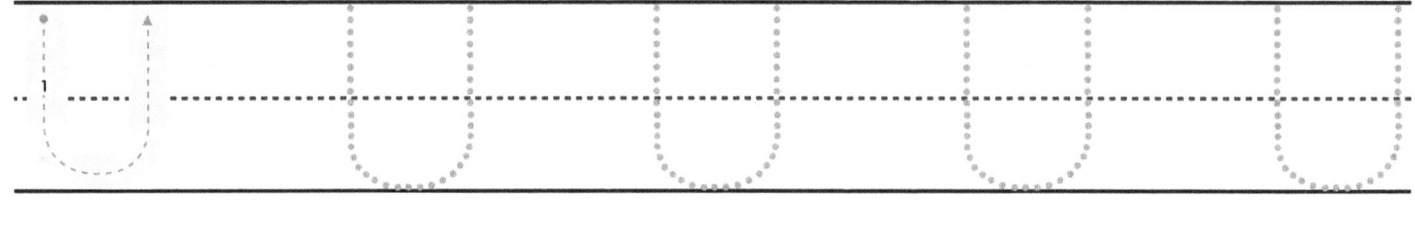

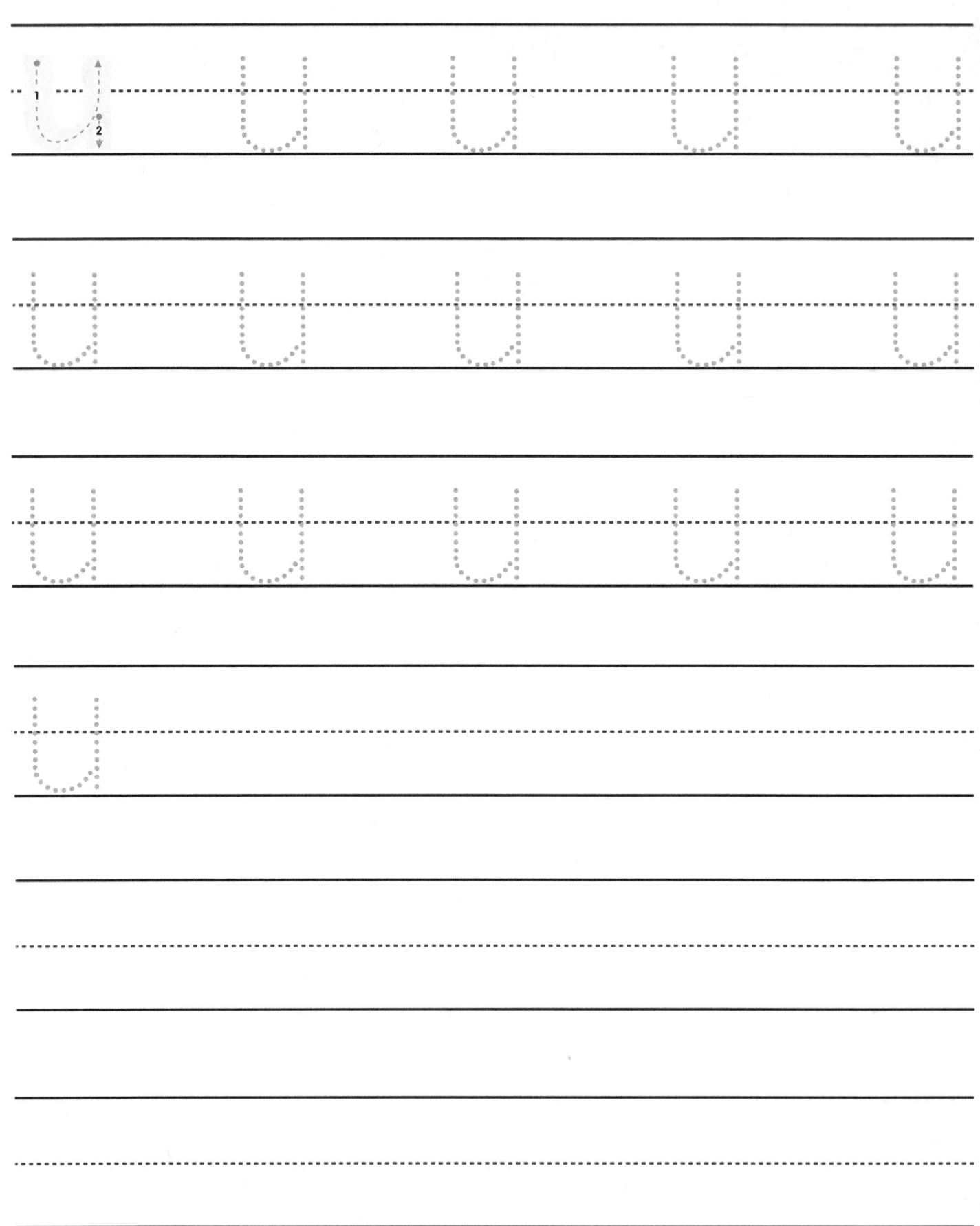

V is for
Vervet
monkey

vervet mokey

vervet mokey

vervet mokey

vervet mokey

W is for

Worm

worm worm

worm worm

worm worm

X is for
Xerus

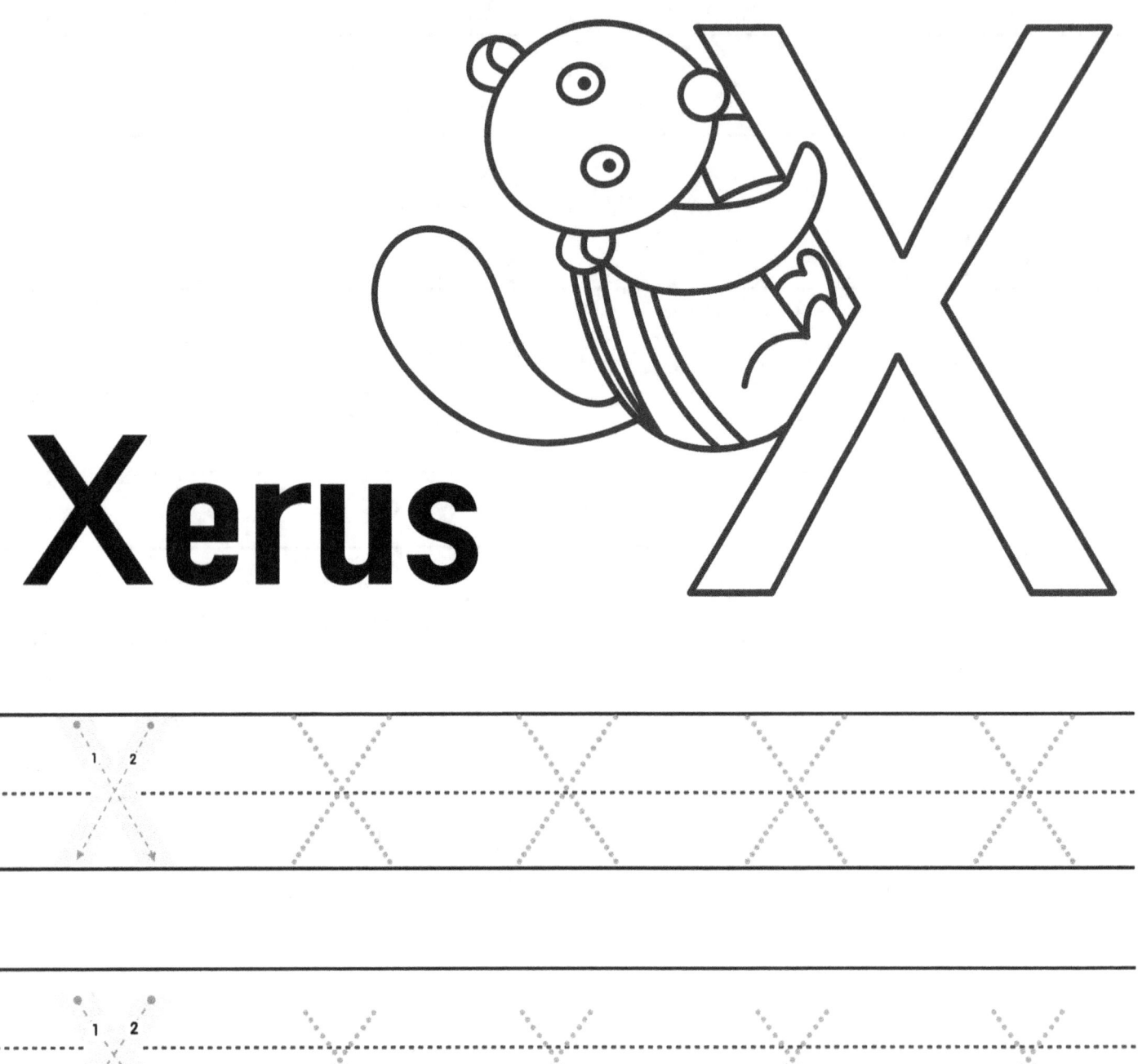

xerus xerus

xerus xerus

xerus xerus

Y is for Yellow baboon

yellow baboon

yellow baboon

yellow baboon

Z is for
Zebu

zebu zebu

zebu zebu

zebu zebu

www.ingramcontent.com/pod-product-compliance
Lightning Source LLC
Chambersburg PA
CBHW081441220526
45466CB00008B/2476